Nonverbal Communications

Body Talk

Written by
Nigel Nelson

Illustrated by
Tony De Saulles

Thomson Learning
New York

Books in the series
Body Talk
Signs and Symbols

First published in the
United States in 1993 by
Thomson Learning
115 Fifth Avenue
New York, NY 10003

First published in 1993 by
Wayland (Publishers) Ltd.

Library of Congress Cataloging-in-Publication Data
Nelson, Nigel
  Body talk / written by Nigel Nelson ; illustrated byTony De Saulles.
      p.   cm. – (Nonverbal communications)
  Includes bibliographical references and index.
  Summary: Introduces ways messages, ideas, and feelings can be
communicated without words.
  ISBN 1-56847-099-1 : $12.95
  1. Nonverbal communication (Psychology) – Juvenile literature.
[1. Nonverbal communication.] I. De Saulles, Tony, ill.
II. Title. III. Series.
BF637.N66N45   1993
153.6'9 – dc20   93-27780

Printed in Italy

Contents

Words that are printed in **bold** are explained in the glossary.

You know what I mean

Look closely at the children in this picture.
How do you think they are feeling or what kind of
mood are they in? How can you tell?

People send messages with their bodies all the time without speaking. You can learn all kinds of things about people by looking at what they do with their bodies.

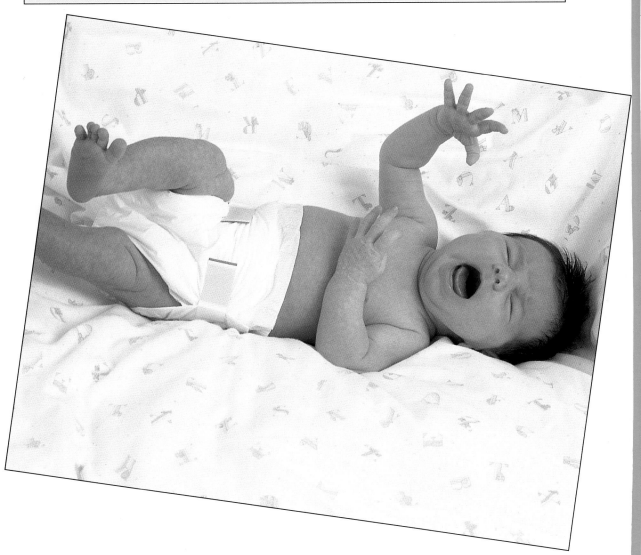

This baby cannot talk. It cries to show that it wants something. Crying usually means that someone is sad or in pain.

Reading faces

You "read" peoples' faces every day. You can often tell how people are feeling by their **expressions**. People all over the world use similar expressions.

Do you think this girl is worried, happy, surprised, or sad? How can you tell?

How do you think this person is feeling? Why do you think that?

What kind of expression does this girl have? What may have happened to make her feel like this?

Activity

Cut out faces from magazines showing different expressions. Put similar or different expressions together to make a collage.

Signs and gestures

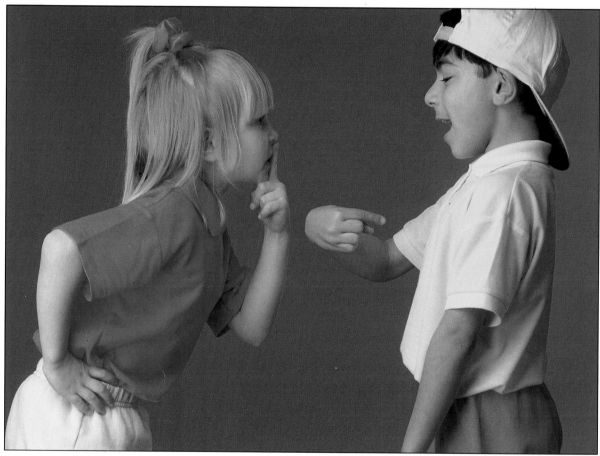

We use signs and **gestures** to explain things more clearly when we are talking. We mostly use our hands and arms. What do you think these children are "saying" with their gestures?

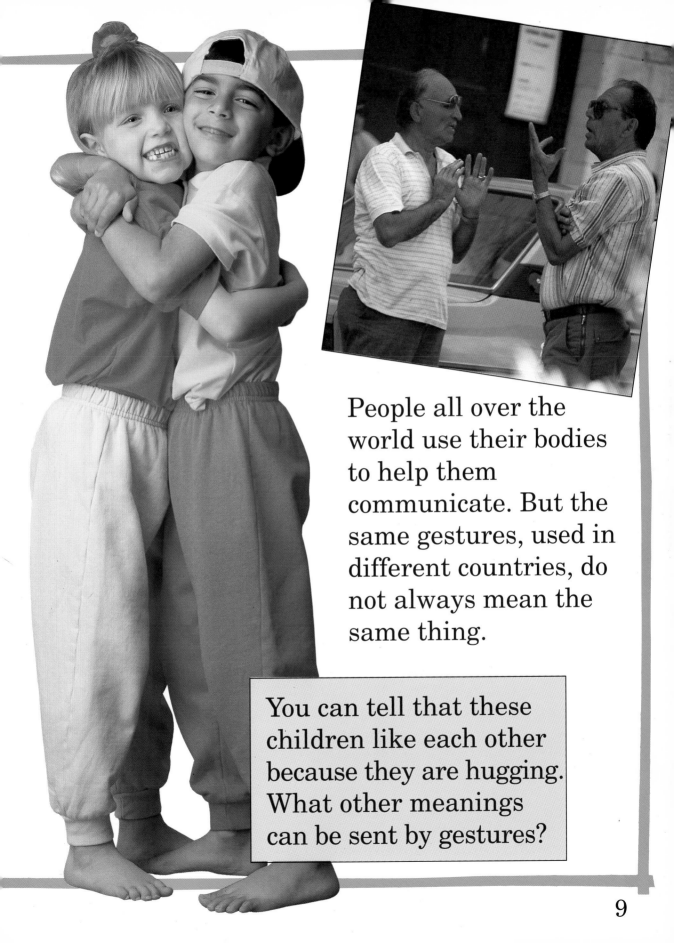

People all over the world use their bodies to help them communicate. But the same gestures, used in different countries, do not always mean the same thing.

You can tell that these children like each other because they are hugging. What other meanings can be sent by gestures?

Body decoration

In many places people decorate their bodies in special ways. This can often tell you quite a lot about them.

Sometimes people decorate their bodies because they want to look different.

Members of the **Rastafarian** religion wear their hair in a special way, like this man.

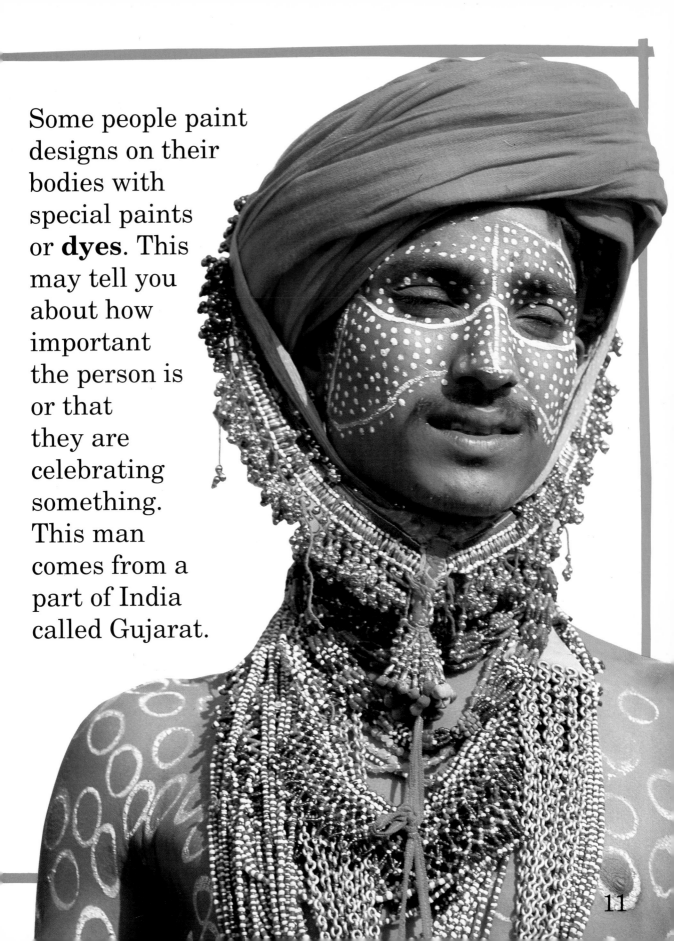

Some people paint designs on their bodies with special paints or **dyes**. This may tell you about how important the person is or that they are celebrating something. This man comes from a part of India called Gujarat.

Clothes talk

The clothes that people wear can also tell you about them. These children are wearing a uniform to show which school they go to.

Special clothes are worn on special occasions. Bright costumes like these tell us that carnival is a time of happiness and fun. Many people wear special clothes for weddings and **funerals**.

Design a T-shirt
that shows people
something you feel
strongly about.

Some people wear clothes that send a message
with words or pictures.
This is often to
show that they
support a
special group
or have certain
beliefs.

13

Animal signals

The colors and patterns of some animals send signals and messages to other animals. Many creatures are have special colors or patterns that help them to hide from danger. This is called camouflage. This chameleon can change the color of its body for camouflage.

Other creatures have bright colors that act as a warning. The black and yellow stripes of this wasp are a sign to other creatures that it can sting.

Activity

Find out about other creatures. What is the best camouflage you know of? What makes it best?

Animal communications

Most animals send messages to each other. They use body movements, sounds, and even smell.

When a cat is happy and calm it closes its eyes and purrs.

This cat is scared and angry. It is arching its back and spitting.

Just like people, chimpanzees and other apes have a lot of different expressions. They use these expressions to send messages to each other.

On the stage

Some people are very good at using their bodies to tell stories. These actors are using their bodies to help explain what is happening in a Japanese play.

A mime is an actor who does not use his or her voice at all. These mimes have painted their faces and are using actions to describe what is happening in their play.

Activity

Make masks that show different expressions. Use your body to mime the expression. Make up a play using the characters you create.

Dance

In every country of the world people like to dance.

Some traditional dances tell a story. These dancers from Bali move their hands and bodies in special ways. Each movement has a meaning.

Activity Design a way to tell one of your favorite stories using body movement or dance.

Sports signals

In many sports the **referee** uses special signals to explain what is happening. This helps the players as well as the people watching. This football referee is signaling a touchdown.

At the end of a **Thai boxing** match, the referee holds up the arm of one of the boxers to show that she is the winner.

This soccer player is being shown a yellow card. This is a signal to the player and the audience that he has been warned about breaking the rules.

Instructions

Some body talk has very strict rules. It is usually used by people giving **instructions**. Police officers use special signals to direct the traffic.

The **conductor** of an **orchestra** uses a special stick called a baton to signal to the musicians. The musicians know what each movement means. By watching the signals they can play the music correctly.

Hand signals made by a cyclist are a way of telling other road users what the cyclist is going to do. Find out what these signals are. Do they make sense to you?

Religious signs

There are many different religions in the world. Some religious people make special signs and gestures with their bodies.

Muslims, like these people in China, face the holy city of Mecca when they pray. They kneel down and bend forward so that their foreheads touch the ground.

Many **Christians** make the sign of the cross with their hands. People from many religions put their hands together when they pray.

All together

Sometimes many people speak together without talking! When the people in an audience clap and whistle they are saying "thank you" and "good job." The people in this picture are making a giant "wave." It is a way of cheering for their team.

These people are all playing their part in making one big message. Each person holds up one piece of a giant cardboard puzzle. At a signal, they turn over their pieces to make a different picture.

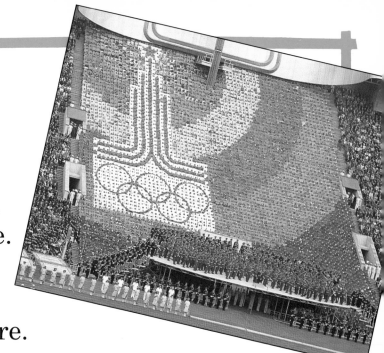

Activity

Make your own giant two-sided puzzle.
1. Paint a picture on each side of a large piece of cardboard.
2. Cut it up into equal squares.
3. Mix up the pieces and then see if you can put together one picture, and then the other.

Glossary

Christians People who believe in Jesus Christ and his teachings.

Conductor The leader of an orchestra or choir.

Dye A liquid used to color something.

Expression A look that can show how someone is feeling.

Funeral The special events that take place when somebody has died.

Gestures Body movements that tell you something.

Instructions Ways of saying exactly how to do something.

Muslims People who believe in the religion of Islam.

Orchestra A group of people, playing different instruments, who come together to make music.

Rastafarian A member of a religious group that developed in Jamaica.

Referee A sports official who makes sure the players follow the rules.

Thai Boxing A type of boxing where the fighters are allowed to use their feet as well as their hands.

Books to read

Bailey, Donna. *Dancing.* Sports World. Austin: Raintree Steck-Vaughn, 1991.

Burnie, David. *Communication.* Animal Behavior. New York: Gloucester Press, 1992.

Kalman, Bobbie. *How We Communicate.* New York: Crabtree Publishing Co., 1986.

Mayes, Susan. *How Do Animals Talk?.* Tulsa: EDC Publishing, 1991.

Nelson, Nigel. *Signs and Symbols.* Nonverbal Communications. New York: Thomson Learning, 1993.

Weil, Lisl. *New Clothes: What People Wore – From Cavemen to Astronauts.* New York: Macmillan Children's Book Group, 1987.

Picture acknowledgments

The publishers would like to thank the following for allowing their photographs to be reproduced in this book: Action Plus Photographic 22 (Mike Hewitt); All Sport 29 (Tony Duffy); Bruce Coleman Ltd., 15 (above/Jane Burton); Daniel Pangbourne *cover*, 6 (both), 7, 8, 9 (left), 13, 19 (below); Eye Ubiquitous 9 (right/Paul Seheult), 12 (below), 16 (above/Paul Prestidge), 25 (below/Mostyn), 26 (Julia Waterlow), 27 (Skjold); Life File 20 (Jeremy Hoare); Photri 16 (below); Press Association/Topham Picture Library 28; Reflections 5 (Jennie Woodcock); Tony Stone Worldwide 17, 21 (Thierry Cazabon); Wayland Picture Library 10 (below), 18, 19 (above).

Index